Praise for
30 Days to What Matters

. . .

"In this fast paced world it's so easy to lose sight of what's important. Being able to slow down and reflect on what really matters is a treasure. This journal creates that opportunity."
- Pastor Matty Coppin

"Getting clear on what truly matters to us is no easy feat! Finding the values that resonate with us and represent our inner compass can be a confusing yet liberating process. If we want to live our lives authentically, tuning into our values is absolutely essential. Danielle's warm, honest, and knowledgeable encouragement turns what can be a daunting process into one of refreshing self-exploration and unrealized potential. Working through this brave journal will provoke novel thoughts, nudge a colourful palate of feelings, and guide readers towards renewed clarity and an acceptance of the values that help lead us to live lives grounded in What Matters."
- Christine Sribney, R.Psych.

"Danielle Reed reminds us that our values are the foundation of our character. She teaches that upon this foundation we can intentionally construct our lives using our words, thoughts, insights, and energies as the materials. Her 30 days journal will guide you. no matter what age, to establish your four ~~~~~~ ~~~~~~ perfectly practice the habits that you'll ne~ were meant to live."
- Derek Peterson, International

This book is a beautiful way to uncomplicate life's more challenging lessons. By uncovering the values that guide our daily decisions, there is a truthful simplicity revealed and a deeper understanding of one's self as well as those around us.

- Tammy Schepens, Assistant Principal

Danielle Reed's personal calling as a group life coach shines through beautifully in her 30 Days Journal. Her *What Matters Values* work is life changing in approaching the common human struggles of "Where Have I gone Wrong?", "Why Can't I Find Happiness?" and where it shows up in my office - "What's Wrong me Doctor - I'm Sad and Anxious all the time." Danielle has become our local icon in this type of work. Here in this journal, she simplifies the use of these values, using stories from previous clients and quotes from great teachers in the field to help on one's journey to live the best life for each of us.

- Elizabeth Dixon MD CCFP Family Physician
Special Interest in Women's Medicine

This book is amazing! As a coach, I am familiar with values but the way that Danielle presents and uses them is so refreshing! She really helps you connect on a deep level to yourself and your life. I LOVED Nolan's contribution. It shows how we can practically help the next generation love and appreciate themselves and move through life confidently and compassionately. Oh and one more thing…. the stories that are throughout the book are incredible! Buy this book and discover what really matters to you and start living your life in a whole new way!! You won't regret it!"

- Tamara Vanlint, Coach

I love Danielle's journal! This beautiful book guides you on a journey to discover your deepest core values to give you a compass to intentionally create a life in which your actions align with your values. When I first started exploring my values, I was overwhelmed. Danielle has created a mangeable process for uncovering what matters most in order to create a life that is a reflection of your authentic self. With a practicable daily focus coupled with engaging stories you create a deeper connection to self which translates to all of your relationships. As a couples therapist, I intend to use this journal to guide couples toward a deeper understanding and acceptance of each other.

-Kim Dean JD, MA Clinical Psychology (candidate), Life Coach

My dear Cousin Melanie
It is up to you: only you!

To create the life you want,
to live each day surrounded
by what brings you happiness!
Much love: laughter
Always.
Cousin
Dodi

Follow Your
Own Path
&
Your People
Will Find
You

ISBN: 978-1-988675-28-2

First Edition: October 2017

STOKE Publishing

to Nolan & Spencer
for being my greatest teachers
and for choosing to be
exactly who you are
I love you!

Introduction

It took me 37 years to figure out who I am and what truly mattered to me. I spent a lot of years focused on accomplishments and trying the next big thing, thinking that somehow the trophies, medals and recognition would bring me happiness.

I couldn't have been further from the truth.

The more I achieved, the more I pushed myself, and the more unhappy I became.

Somehow my self-worth was attached to all of my successes. But if I wasn't happy, why did any of them matter?

In 2008, my life came crumbling down.

I was left asking myself two key questions:
1. What truly matters to me?
2. What example am I being to my kids?

I set off on a journey to separate myself from my accomplishments, to dig deep into who I was and what mattered to me, and in doing so I found the person I am today.

I found my most authentic self.

Answering the first question - What truly matters to me? - was not an easy thing to do, but it was worth it.

The absolute key to answering this question was finding my top values and choosing to live in alignment with them. Choosing a life of intention.

What I realized was that I was living a life that did not reflect my key values. I had stepped off the path of what mattered to me, and when we do that, depression, anxiety, lack of fulfillment and unhappiness show up. You see, our values are like an internal compass. They are trying to point us in the right direction. They are trying to show us our most authentic selves. We get to choose to listen to and follow that compass or we can ignore it.

My compass was pointing me toward my key values:
Authenticity
Balance
Connection
Gratitude
Humor
Health
Learning
Legacy
Organization
Optimism
Understanding

The day that I found these values, I felt like I found myself.

If I could live these values each and every day life would be amazing.

So I began. With intention, I started each day on the edge of my bed saying each word aloud and visualizing what it may look like that day. I did the same to end my days, I would sit on the edge of my bed, say my values aloud and evaluate whether or not I was true to each value that day. I also practiced self-compassion. On the days when one of them seemed like it was missing, I asked myself one question, "How can you live that value more fully tomorrow?"

There is so much more than simply saying I know my values. Practicing them each day takes work and intention until one day it just becomes who you are.

Today, I don't have to sit on my bed and recite them to myself. They are in my mind every moment of each day. In fact, if I notice my mood turn from great to crappy I simply stop and realign. I ask myself, "What value is not being honored right now?" and very quickly I can turn a crappy moment back into a great day.

Finding my top values and choosing to live them with intention changed my life. I had never felt happiness like this before.

Answering the second question - What example am I being to my kids? - was my WHY.

It is the reason I decided to live a life with intention connected to what matters most to me.

I wanted my kids to see that life doesn't have to be hard, stressful and filled with unhappiness. I wanted to teach them that finding your values and choosing to practice them each and every day is one of the greatest gifts you can give yourself. I wanted them to grow up knowing exactly who they are without this unhealthy hunger for medals, trophies and accomplishments.
I wanted them to be exactly who they are. I wanted them to follow their own compasses.

I did the values work with my husband and boys years ago. My boys were 6 and 9 years old at the time (they are now 13 and 16). It was one of the most amazing discussions I have ever had. We have a What Matters™ wall painted in our kitchen with each of our lists of values on it. It has been the greatest thing to build deeper connection and compassion in our house.

When we argue, we look at each other's values to see which ones are colliding. And we find ways to honor the values in each other.

We use our values to help us make decisions and understand each other.

We use our values to remind us to practice curiosity and compassion over judgment.

I have seen my boys filling out application forms for work or volunteering or as they complete Who Am I type activities for health classes, and they are at the wall using their value words to explain who they are.

At the end of the day, I want to lead by example. I want to show my kids that life can be filled with happiness when you follow your compass and choose to be exactly who you are.

The best advice I can give you is to give it a try. Find your key values, choose to live them with intention and see what happens. And when you realize how amazing it feels, share it with the people you love.

Take your time. Listen to your heart. Just begin.

How to Use this Book

There isn't really a right way or a wrong way to use this journal, but let me give you a few tips:

1. Listen to your heart as your work through it. Write whatever comes to you without judgment.

2. Days 1-27 can be done in any order....just leave Days 28-30 for the end, as they will pull it all together.

3. Each Day is organized around a set of value words. Reflect on each one separately and then ask yourself if any of them matter to you. Do you feel pulled by one or more in particular? Notice where there is resonance.

4. If none of them feel resonant, then move on....well, read the amazing story at the end and then move on to the next day.

5. For the ones that feel resonant, write what a 10/10 day would look like for you if you were living that value.
Example:
For me, BALANCE has resonance.
A 10/10 day would look like this:
I would eat 2/3 meals with my family at the table.
I would work a maximum of 3 evenings per week.
I would go to the gym or yoga 5/7 days.
I would have a feeling of inner peace that all the things that mattered in my life were given the proper amount of attention.

6. Pay attention to which value words are really pulling you. Even if they feel impossible to live right now...if you want them, it's time to take action.

7. Our values are like an internal compass...they are trying to show us the way to our true self. When we listen to and follow the compass, life feels pretty darn awesome! When we ignore it, we feel anxious, depressed, unhappy, disconnected and blah!

8. Even if a value is pulling you, and you feel like it's impossible...put it on your list. For years, I thought living with balance was never going to happen. However, that left me feeling really empty most days. I would wake up with this pit in the stomach feeling of unrest and I'd go to bed with the same feeling. When I intentionally chose to put balance on my list, I began to make small steps toward it and everything changed.

9. Take time to read each of the incredible stories sprinkled throughout the book. After each one, reflect on one key learning you will take away after reading that story.

9. Once you have completed Days 1-27, you will have a much better sense of what values truly matter to you. Allow yourself time to sit with them before you jump into Days 28-30. Notice your best days...which values are present? Notice your moments of frustration....which values are missing?

10. Day 28 is getting clear about what your values are and what each word means to you. We are all different. If asked to explain respect, every person may have a slightly different opinion of what that looks like to them and what they need. As you write your manifesto, allow yourself to dig deeper into what that value really means to YOU!

11. Day 29 is a check in. How aligned are you with the values that matter to you? Which ones are you living? Which ones need more attention? Most importantly, how can you move forward with greater intention?

12. Day 30 is putting the values into action. This is where you choose to practice your values each and every day!

Foreward

By Nolan Reed

I remember when my mom did my values with me at nine years old. I had no idea at the time how knowing my values would impact my life. I remember the word authenticity, and this idea of being myself was something I really wanted. This word acted as my guide throughout junior high and into high school. This idea that I could be exactly who I am, and not have to change for anyone was so important to me. I also started to realize that the more I was myself, the more I found friends who liked me for exactly who I was, and these were the kind of people I wanted to hang out with.

Another key value for me is family. It's always been important to me. I really enjoy spending time with family, and always want to be sure I make time for them. When my Papa passed away last year, I really realized how much family meant to me. He was such an important part of my life, and the way our family came together at such a difficult time was something I will never forget.

A value I didn't realize mattered so much was responsibility. I like to volunteer, do well in school and basically, act like a decent human being. This value helps guide my decisions each day.

If I could give advice to anyone, I would tell them to find and choose to live by your values because it gives you permission to be yourself, and it brings the right people into your life.

I'm grateful that my mom helped me to find What Matters™ at such a young age because it has shaped who I am today.

"Be yourself because the people who mind don't matter, and the people that matter don't mind."

Dr.Seuss

DAY 1

Value words to focus on for today:
Authenticity
Uniqueness
Confidence

Sit in silence and think about what each of these words means to you. Jot down your thoughts or write your own definition of each word:

Authenticity -

Uniqueness -

Confidence -

Circle any word(s) that resonates for you:
Authenticity   Uniqueness   Confidence

If none of the above words resonate for you...move on to day 2.

What would a 10/10 day look like living this value?
Describe it in as much detail as you can.
Write, doodle, draw, be as creative as you wish.

Living with Values
by Kendra Regimbald

I truly believe that being authentic is one of the most beautiful things we have been given, and we have all been made unique for a reason. However, I haven't always felt this way. Growing up I felt like I lived in a society where being authentic, and truly being "me" was socially unaccepted and looked down on. I really struggled growing up with not feeling comfortable about being who I was, not because I was ashamed or embarrassed, more like I had to pretend I was just like every other girl in junior high; which never truly made me feel content. When I branched out and learned more about myself and my values, I started seeing people in my life who also knew their values. No matter who they were with or what they were doing they just seemed to live so fully and authentically. This sparked a fire inside me, giving me courage and inspiration to be my true self. When I started to understand my values, I realized that I was allowed to love the band Mumford and Sons when every other girl my age loved One Direction, and ever since the moment I realized I could do this I have lived so differently. Understanding my values has made life so much more easy to live. I still go through ups and downs just like everyone else, but I understand myself better, and I know how to help myself when I am not happy. I understand why I like things and why I don't, I understand why some relationships work in my life and why some don't. Most importantly it's helped me understand myself. It has helped me understand that I am the way I am because of what I value in life. It has helped my relationships; understanding and respecting the similarities and differences between our values makes all the difference. It also helps me seek out other authentic people who know and respect their values. Understanding my values has helped me make more sense of who I am. Most importantly, it has helped me love and embrace my true self and to love others for who they truly are as well.

Reflection:
What is ONE key learning that you can you take
away from this story?

"You can choose courage
or you can choose
comfort,
but you cannot have
both."

Brené Brown

DAY 2

Value words to focus on for today:
Adventure
Freedom
Courage

Sit in silence and think about what each of these words means to you. Jot down your thoughts or write your own definition of each word:

Adventure -

Freedom -

Courage -

Circle any word(s) that resonates for you:

Adventure   Freedom   Courage

If none of the above words resonate for you...move on to day 3.

What would a 10/10 day look like living this value?
Describe it in as much detail as you can.
Write, doodle, draw, be as creative as you wish.

The Courage to Be Me
by Austin Thomas Whittle

Why should I be anyone other then me? This question is easier said than done because on plenty of occasions I have betrayed this value. Personally my problems with embracing who I am began in middle school. Unlike other students who began to change during this time I kept my values and because of this I began to become more out of touch with my friends. While I still loved to play games and watch movies my friends began to prefer sports and partying. However hard I tried, it seemed I couldn't find a way to keep childhood friendships together and slowly my friends began to surround themselves with people who I couldn't relate to. Luckily I did some life-coaching with Danielle Reed and she helped me to realize that I wasn't obsolete and that my friendship's failings had little to do with me. These talks where integral because they acted as the foundation of my future lifestyle and personality. Danielle believed that I should try to find new friends; friends who I had more in common with instead of trying to fit in with my old friends. At the time I wasn't truly invested in this idea, but slowly I began to recognize some friends I never knew I had. By grade ten I was starting to be included in a new group of friends and I was happy. While around my new friends I felt encouraged to be authentic, and I was beginning to receive invitations to spend time with them, which had become almost a foreign idea. Because of the authenticity that Danielle encouraged me to embrace, high school has been the best three years of my life which is a surprising contrast to middle school. Today I regret the fact that I stalled from following my values because I believe I could have loved middle school equivalently to high school if I had acted sooner.

Reflection:
What is ONE key learning that you can you take away from this story?

"Humor is mankind's greatest blessing."

Mark Twain

DAY 3

Value words to focus on for today:
Silliness
Humor

Sit in silence and think about what each of these words means to you. Jot down your thoughts or write your own definition of each word:

Silliness -

Humor -

Circle any word(s) that resonates for you:
Silliness　　　　　　　Humor

If none of the above words resonate for you...move on to day 4.

What would a 10/10 day look like living this value?
Describe it in as much detail as you can.
Write, doodle, draw, be as creative as you wish.

Permission to Be Silly
by Leah F.

Doing Values work with my family has been so enlightening. I'll never forget the day my daughter picked her top ten values. She was nine at the time. We laid all the What Matters™ cards out on our table and she went through each of them selecting any that caught her interest right away. We then took that pile and went through each one. Some she knew had to be in her top ten right away and others she would sit and think about. She also grouped similar words together and we would talk about each of them and then very decidedly she would choose the one she knew was right for her. My husband, son and I all have humor in our top values. We all love to joke and laugh and this didn't surprise me it would show up. My daughter was torn between humor and silliness. She sat with both cards for a minute. I didn't want to push her to pick humor, but I was positive that she would choose it over silliness. Then, very matter of factly she said, "It's silliness for me". I asked her why she chose silliness over humor. She said, "It is much more important to me to be silly than funny." It was such a pivotal point for me in parenting her. I didn't often have patience for her silliness, but when I realized how important it was to her I knew I had to honor that value in her. I don't value silliness, but I have to respect that it is important to her and this gives me so much more patience for her silliness now. I love to see her light up when she's being silly and truly being herself. This realization has made me appreciate the difference in our values as well as letting her be her own person, not a mini version of myself.

Reflection:
What is ONE key learning that you can you take
away from this story?

"Nothing ever goes away until it teaches us what we need to know."

Pema Chödrön

DAY 4

Value words to focus on for today:
Wisdom
Intelligence
Learning
Curiosity

Sit in silence and think about what each of these words means to you. Jot down your thoughts or write your own definition of each word:

Wisdom -

Intelligence -

Learning -

Curiosity -

Circle any word(s) that resonates for you:
Wisdom   Intelligence   Learning   Curiosity

If none of the above words resonate for you...move on to day 5.

What would a 10/10 day look like living this value?
Describe it in as much detail as you can.
Write, doodle, draw, be as creative as you wish.

Meeting Myself for the First Time
by Sharon Milroy

I was going through life methodically. Going to work, making dinner, laundry, cleaning and driving kids around. I knew deep down something was wrong though, but it was just too scary to look at it in the eyes. I skirted around it, I avoided it. I simply didn't want to face it. I loved the idea of a "Women's Wellness Evening" that Danielle was offering. I can do that, I thought; one day a month to myself. I deserve that … and there will be wine! Maybe, I'm ready to look inwards. It was a safe place and a slow pace. What happened since then has changed my life. What profound questions Danielle asked. What life altering answers came out of my own mouth. I had an "AHA" moment. My fog cleared so quickly for me and the clarity I felt was powerful. I had known it all along. I had unconsciously been mourning it for years. I was finally ready to look it in the eyes. It came down to my values. "What are your core values?" Danielle asked me. I had never been asked that before. Not as a child, not as a young adult and never as a middle aged wife and mother of three. I didn't know my own values. How incredibly sad. When I did finally dig up my true core values, I sat staring at the words and started to cry. Authenticity, Connection, Creativity, Peace, Humor and Balance. It was like meeting myself for the first time. The words felt so familiar and kind to me, yet I was not being true to any one of them. No wonder I felt so estranged with myself. I have changed my life since then. A massive, upside down, shift in direction - kind of change. It has been the hardest thing I have ever done. On the other hand, I feel so true to myself and my core values that I know it was the right thing to do. I since speak of values often with my children, I ask them if they are being true to theirs in all the decisions they make. I would never want them to land so far away from theirs, and I will never let myself do that again.

Reflection:
What is ONE key learning that you can you take
away from this story?

"Integrity is doing the right thing. Even when no one is watching."

C.S.Lewis

DAY 5

Value words for today:
Integrity
Ethics
Truth
Honesty
Trust
Loyalty

Sit in silence and think about what each of these words means to you.
Jot down your thoughts or write your own definition of each word:

Integrity-

Ethics -

Truth -

Honesty -

Trust -

Loyalty -

Circle any word(s) that resonates for you:

Integrity   Ethics   Truth   Honesty   Trust   Loyalty

If none of the above words resonate for you...move on to day 6.

What would a 10/10 day look like living this value?
Describe it in as much detail as you can.
Write, doodle, draw, be as creative as you wish.

Standing in My Integrity
Anonymous Author

My top three values are respect, compassion and integrity. I feel so empowered when I stand behind those words. I feel self worth, and I feel that I am living an authentic life.

My story…I started a new business adventure in a creative field. I had to put myself out there for critique and evaluation. I was elated and so grateful for the opportunity to do business with a certain company. At the time, I would do whatever it took to make this a successful venture. As time went on this one company became increasingly hard to deal with. They were rude and totally disrespectful. But the problem or so it seemed at the time was that they were making money for me. The business side of it was successful, but the relationship was not. I ignored how they treated me. I told myself I didn't have to like them. I never responded emotionally to their rude emails or phone calls. I kept my cool. I thought I was doing well. My body was telling me another story … I started feeling sick to my stomach when I had to contact them on business matters. I started rewriting emails several times and keeping them in my inbox to reread later to make sure I said just the right thing. Trying not to upset anyone. I realized I was not living my values. Nothing felt right. I wanted to leave this business partnership, but I was telling myself, maybe this is as good as it gets, maybe I just have to be tougher. At some point I decided, on purpose, to live my values. I decided to be compassionate to myself. I decided to respect myself and make choices based on integrity. I decided to stand up for what I believed in. I treat people in my life with these values, but it was a big moment to uphold these values for myself. I made a decision to leave. No matter what the outcome…I felt empowered. When I live my values, the universe has my back!

Reflection:
What is ONE key learning that you can you take away from this story?

"Creativity is a crushing chore and a glorious mystery. The work wants to be made, and it wants to be made through you."

Elizabeth Gilbert

DAY 6

Value words for today:
Imagination
Creativity

Sit in silence and think about what each of these words means to you.
Jot down your thoughts or write your own definition of each word:

Imagination-

Creativity -

Circle any word(s) that resonates for you:
Imagination   Creativity

If none of the above words resonate for you...move on to day 7.

What would a 10/10 day look like living this value?
Describe it in as much detail as you can.
Write, doodle, draw, be as creative as you wish.

I was Born with a Creative Spirit
By Vicki

Understanding my core values and learning how to live my life aligned with who I am and what I believe has been a journey. Determining what my values are was easier that I thought it would be. A simple glance through the list of values words - several quickly stood out as essential and important. Learning how to focus on those values and staying true to who I am has become a daily challenge and a lifelong goal. Understanding my values has helped me to focus on what is important in my work, in my home, and in my relationships. Each year I choose a word to focus on, to remind myself of it's importance. This past year I chose one of my core value words - Creativity - as a key reminder of where to place my soul, energy and time. I was born with a creative spirit. When I paint, make jewelry, engage in paper crafts or even color, I experience "flow". I get lost in time and I feel recharged and whole. I have learned over this past year that making time for my crafts and taking opportunities to learn new skills through art classes keeps me grounded and happy. Before learning about the importance of core values I would get buried in the busyness of life responsibilities. Work and household tasks took over the majority of each day. I would view craft time as idle time, not important and frivolous, I would postpone art projects until the "real" work was done. I knew that I loved it, but I didn't realize that I needed it. I now realize that "to create" is my soul's work. I now not only "allow" myself time to pursue my hobbies, I foster it and schedule it in. Taking time to create allows my soul to wander free. Being creative makes me happy and as a result I am more productive in all other areas of my life.

Reflection:
What is ONE key learning that you can you take away from this story?

"The best way to find yourself is to lose yourself in the service of others."

Mahatma Gandhi

DAY 7

Value words for today:
Helpfulness
Contribution
Service
Altruism
Usefulness

Sit in silence and think about what each of these words means to you. Jot down your thoughts or write your own definition of each word:

Helpfulness -

Contribution -

Service -

Altruism -

Usefulness -

Circle any word(s) that resonates for you:
Helpfulness   Contribution   Service   Altruism   Usefulness

If none of the above words resonate for you...move on to day 8.

What would a 10/10 day look like living this value?
Describe it in as much detail as you can.
Write, doodle, draw, be as creative as you wish.

Celebrating the Success of Others

By Kelsey McQueen

I have been on a path of self discovery and part of that included discovering my core values and what I needed to feel fulfilled in my life. I had to ask myself what brought me true joy; what made my heart happy. That answer came easily. One of my core values is altruism. I love helping people and being part of something that will change their lives. As a personal trainer, my job is to help people work on getting healthier in mind and body. Often there are personal struggles on that journey and obstacles to get through. What I love is that we get to do that as a team. I work with people to accomplish their goals and get through the challenges they may face along the way. When I am able to help them achieve their goals, I get to be part of something really beautiful. I get to see their confidence grow along the way, I get to see and feel the pride they have in themselves and ultimately, I get to feel the joy they feel when they accomplish a goal that they have set out for themselves. Being part of someone's personal growth and success is beautiful.

Reflection:
What is ONE key learning that you can you take away from this story?

"Our sense of worthiness –
that critical piece that
gives us access to love and
belonging – lives inside our
story."

Brené Brown

DAY 8

Value words to focus on for today:
Inclusion
Acceptance
Belonging
Patience

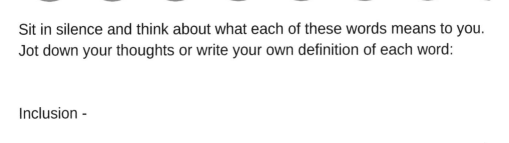

Sit in silence and think about what each of these words means to you. Jot down your thoughts or write your own definition of each word:

Inclusion -

Acceptance-

Belonging -

Patience -

Circle any word(s) that resonates for you:

Inclusion   Acceptance   Belonging   Patience

If none of the above words resonate for you...move on to day 9.

What would a 10/10 day look like living this value? Describe it in as much detail as you can. Write, doodle, draw, be as creative as you wish.

Why Am I Here?
by Alex Flory

I graduated from high school in 2007, from a culture where I was mostly accepted for being me and where I felt I had connections. I spent the next couple of years applying to be accepted in a Post Secondary Program designed for people like me – "Special Needs". When I didn't get accepted the second year, I began taking classes that I enjoyed and had my personal caregiver attend them with me. I spent the next 5 years taking one or two classes each semester. That culture wasn't quite as accepting, but I did manage to make a few acquaintances and loved the atmosphere. Now what… finding a job was an even less inclusive adventure. An employer would have to be able to get past my wheelchair and accept that I had caregivers who needed to come with me to work, while I had to accept that I wouldn't fit into the typical work environment. I began living life from day to day, not even sure why I was here. I felt I had no purpose. I was lacking goals, direction and a job. My daily battle with anxiety was taking its toll on me as well as those around me. Danielle agreed to work with me to clarify my values and strengths. This ultimately led me to realize my life purpose. Today I am a proud business owner. My business and goals are now driven by my values and purpose in life. By including my values in daily life makes me less anxious and more focused. I have overcome many hurdles and challenges that life has thrown my way by simply focusing on why I am here and what lights me up. I have a daily reminder of my values and life purpose that sit on my counter so that I can read them daily. I also keep a gratitude journal to record two reasons I am grateful each day. I have had an overall increase in my mood and a great reduction in stress and anxiety. I can honestly say that learning my values changed the way I see myself.

Reflection:
What is ONE key learning that you can you take
away from this story?

"Joy is what happens to us when we allow ourselves to recognize how good things really are."

Marianne Williamson

DAY 9

Value words to focus on for today:
Happiness
Contentment
Joy

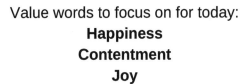

Sit in silence and think about what each of these words means to you. Jot down your thoughts or write your own definition of each word:

Happiness -

Contentment -

Joy-

Circle any word(s) that resonates for you:
Happiness   Contentment   Joy

If none of the above words resonate for you...move on to day 10.

What would a 10/10 day look like living this value?
Describe it in as much detail as you can.
Write, doodle, draw, be as creative as you wish.

Values Bring me Joy
by Hollyanne Healey

Authenticity is my #1 value. To me being authentic means being brave and "honest at all times" in my thoughts, relationships, and life. I lost my Mom to cancer 2 years ago. It was a devastating time. I still feel heartache and loss. I miss her so much every day. My Mother was an amazingly strong, supportive, and courageous woman. She taught me to treasure every day; that life is a precious gift. She always took the time to tell me how much she loved me, every time we spoke. I made a promise to her that I would always remember and take time to love and cherish our family. Trying to do that while working through my grief and sadness was a huge challenge for me. It was at that time that I learned about the importance of living my values. I have come to recognize my need to have honest, true, authentic relationships. I no longer have time or patience to waste on judgment, gossip, and grand standing. These things leave me feeling empty, anxious, and angry inside. I have had to release some unhealthy relationships, but I have gained a clearer understanding of who my people truly are. Today, when my feelings of sadness and grief come around, I know I am going to be okay. I strive to be mindful of the importance of "authenticity" and appreciate everything I have in my life. From my loving wonderful husband, amazing children, supportive friends and family, and our heart-warming community. Authenticity gives me peace, and a feeling of serenity. Now, I speak of my values regularly. At work, when faced with stressful and difficult situations I try to remember and practice my values. They help me handle situations and deal with people in a more patient and understanding way. We speak of our values at home, each one of our family members has their own unique list of values. Knowing and practicing them reminds us to respect each other's differences, while embracing our imperfections. I delight in knowing my values. They make me the person that I am today. They bring me happiness and joy!

Reflection:
What is ONE key learning that you can you take away from this story?

"Compassion is the wish to see others free from suffering."

Dalai Lama

DAY 10

Value words to focus on for today:
Kindness
Compassion
Caring
Generosity

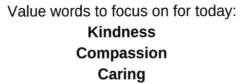

Sit in silence and think about what each of these words means to you.
Jot down your thoughts or write your own definition of each word:

Kindness -

Compassion-

Caring -

Generosity -

Circle any word(s) that resonates for you:
Kindness   Compassion   Caring   Generosity

If none of the above words resonate for you...move on to day 11.

What would a 10/10 day look like living this value?
Describe it in as much detail as you can.
Write, doodle, draw, be as creative as you wish.

The Antidote to Perfection
by Tracy Fisher

I, like many other people (women specifically) have struggled with the need to be perfect. We get sold the idea that somehow our experiences will be richer and that we will be more worthy if we present a polished version of ourselves and our lives. I have worked with many different values exercises over the years and the value that always resonates with me is compassion. I consider compassion; self compassion especially, to be the antidote to perfection. When we offer compassion to ourselves and others, when we can show up in our lives as authentic humans that make mistakes, we get to live a life that has more meaning. The beautiful thing I have found is that when we are compassionate towards ourselves, we more freely extend it to others and it makes the world a little kinder. I work in the wellness industry where self-loathing and negative self talk is prevalent. If negative self talk was the great motivator people think it is, we would all be exactly where we want to be in our lives as so many of us have tried it on! Trust me, it is not an effective strategy. Research shows that when we are kind and compassionate, we are far more likely to become who we truly want to be. Compassion is truly a gift and the best part is, it is a gift you can give yourself over and over again.

Reflection:
What is ONE key learning that you can you take away from this story?

"If you truly love nature, you'll find beauty everywhere."

Vincent Van Gogh

DAY 11

Value words to focus on for today:
Beauty
Nature

Sit in silence and think about what each of these words means to you. Jot down your thoughts or write your own definition of each word:

Beauty-

Nature -

Circle any word(s) that resonates for you:

Beauty　　　　　　　　　Nature

If none of the above words resonate for you...move on to day 12.

What would a 10/10 day look like living this value?
Describe it in as much detail as you can.
Write, doodle, draw, be as creative as you wish.

Nature Fills My Soul

by Jennifer Sparks
Life Strategist SWIFTKICKlife.com

Determining my values and living in alignment with them has changed my life and understanding my values has made sense of some of the most unsettled times of my life. One of my values focuses on immersion in, and connection with nature. Prior to truly having this identified for myself, I had moved through one of the most trying times in my life by spending time outdoors running. Time on the trails, hiding deep in the trees fed my soul in ways I just couldn't get from anything else. Connection to nature is how I refueled. It is where I was awe struck with gratitude for this amazing world I live in. In a way, it was my Church. Only, I didn't really know it yet.

Flash-forward to a time when I lost this connection with nature and this unidentified value slipped to the bottom of my priority list. My stress increased. I was unhappy. I was often exhausted. And, I was losing my grip on gratitude as well. Then, I did a values activity and clearly identified connection with nature as one of my core values. I reflected on this value and thought back to the time when I was living in alignment with this need. Life was not always awesome but living in alignment with that value made everything in my life better. When I slipped and stopped valuing this part of who I was, I lost a grip on many other things in my life as well. Understanding this, I incorporated time in nature back into my calendar. I scheduled time with my "Church" almost on the daily. I kayaked, walked the dog along the river, sat in the park and took meditative walks in the trees. Inhaling the smell of the leaves in the fall and the damp earthy dirt brought me into the now. Taking snowy walks listening to the muffled silence all around me, admiring the sparkling frost, and listening to the snow crunching under my feet slowed my thinking down. Stopping to feel the sun on my face or inhale the scent of a fresh rain fills my soul and is where I am most myself and at peace with all that is in my life.

Reflection:
What is ONE key learning that you can you take
away from this story?

"Fairness is not giving everyone the same thing. Fairness is giving each person what they need to succeed."

Rick Lavoie

DAY 12

Value words for today:
Equality
Diversity
Fairness

Sit in silence and think about what each of these words means to you.
Jot down your thoughts or write your own definition of each word:

Equality -

Diversity -

Fairness -

Circle any word(s) that resonates for you:
Equality   Diversity   Fairness

If none of the above words resonate for you...move on to day 13.

What would a 10/10 day look like living this value?
Describe it in as much detail as you can.
Write, doodle, draw, be as creative as you wish.

Fairness Matters
Anonymous Author

I frequently find my values are most evident when they have been crossed.
I had a situation at work that I found extremely unfair. When my attempt to
rectify the situation was met with anger, I had a loud and heated argument with
a colleague. I was surprised by my own anger and the intensity of my
emotions. It took me a few days to process the situation, but what I discovered
is that fairness is extremely important to me. So if I, my children or my patients
have been treated unfairly, I need to speak and advocate.
Now when I sense my fairness value is being trampled on by someone else, I
ask for clarification and speak sooner than later. I can also offer myself
compassion when life is unfair and I can't create change, instead of ruminating
about those circumstances for days; which frees me up to live my other values.

Reflection:
What is ONE key learning that you can you take
away from this story?

"Faith includes noticing the mess, the emptiness and discomfort, and letting it be there until some light returns."

Anne Lamott

DAY 13

Value words for today:
Faith
Reflection
Spirituality

Sit in silence and think about what each of these words means to you.
Jot down your thoughts or write your own definition of each word:

Faith-

Reflection -

Spirituality -

Circle any word(s) that resonates for you:
Faith   Reflection   Spirituality

If none of the above words resonate for you...move on to day 14.

What would a 10/10 day look like living this value?
Describe it in as much detail as you can.
Write, doodle, draw, be as creative as you wish.

Allowing Faith to Take Center Stage
By Jenine Perrott

Faith~ trusting in something we can't explicitly prove.
For me, Faith has been beautiful, comforting and necessary. It has been tested many times in my life. Most recently when our beautiful daughter told us she was gay. We had many heart to heart discussions, and many personal hurdles were overcome. What I know to be true is this; a mother's love is deep and fierce. Sometimes that love can turn into fear. We fear the world will be unkind to our children. I was never afraid of our girl, I was afraid for her. I've come to realize that she is my world. When I accept and love all of her, the world sees this and things begin to shift. As a mom, my struggle wasn't that she was different, it was wondering whether she was going to be okay. At times like this you have to allow faith to take center stage. It's not always easy to believe, especially as a parent. For me, it sometimes feels like it's all I've got. I once heard someone say that you can't pray and worry. It's an insult to God. Just pray and know he's got you. My faith has only deepened lately because of this experience. Little miracles like people, books and perspectives have come to surface. All beautiful, comforting and necessary.

Reflection:
What is ONE key learning that you can you take
away from this story?

"**Play with pride;
win with humility;
lose with dignity.**"

Jim Ashley

DAY 14

Value words for today:
Dignity
Pride

Sit in silence and think about what each of these words means to you. Jot down your thoughts or write your own definition of each word:

Dignity -

Pride -

Circle any word(s) that resonates for you:
Dignity   Pride

If none of the above words resonate for you...move on to day 15.

What would a 10/10 day look like living this value?
Describe it in as much detail as you can.
Write, doodle, draw, be as creative as you wish.

You Can't Fool Yourself

By Anonymous Author

I have a dear friend who I have known for many years. I love everything about him. He's fun, hilarious and has a heart of gold. There was one thing that I didn't understand about him until he told me his values one day. The thing I didn't understand was his frustration with people around him when they did something embarrassing, goofy or incorrect. At the time, I thought maybe he struggled with perfectionism, but something inside me knew there was more to it. One evening, we were sitting around and we pulled out the What Matters™ values cards. Reluctantly, he agreed to do his values. As he went through the cards, he instantly gravitated to one word and said without a doubt, that this was one of his values. The card was pride & dignity. It was like a light bulb went off for me. Of course pride and dignity mattered to him. A while later, I asked him to explain what that meant to him and he told me this:

"Pride and dignity matter to me because to me, you need both of those to have self-respect. If you believe in what you say and do and how you act and treat others you know that you are a good person. Some people put on a false front and fool others into thinking they are a good person, but you can't fool yourself. At the end of the day, having pride in what you do, who you are and how you treat others is all that truly matters. I can hold my head high knowing that."

I am so grateful I dug a little deeper. I am so grateful that I didn't just assume he needed life to be perfect. I am so grateful I asked him what mattered and then went a step further to find out why. You will never regret digging deeper with those who matter to you.

Reflection:
What is ONE key learning that you can you take
away from this story?

"Today I shall behave,
as if this is the day
I will be remembered."

Dr.Seuss

DAY 15

Value words for today:
Legacy
Making a Difference

Sit in silence and think about what each of these words means to you.
Jot down your thoughts or write your own definition of each word:

Legacy -

Making a Difference -

Circle any word(s) that resonates for you:
Legacy   Making a Difference

If none of the above words resonate for you...move on to day 16.

What would a 10/10 day look like living this value?
Describe it in as much detail as you can.
Write, doodle, draw, be as creative as you wish.

Papa
by Spencer & Danielle Reed

I'm not sure we always know the legacy someone is leaving completely until they are gone. We love them. We see all their goodness, but we don't always stop to acknowledge it as a legacy.

We were blessed with this amazing Papa and father-in-law. He was such an incredible person, and his death left a hole in the lives of anyone who knew him. Keith stood for family, community and generosity.

He loved our family more than anything. Spending time with his grandchildren was the highlight of his day.

He was so proud of our community and he would do anything to support those in the community who needed it.

He was also incredibly generous. He would sneak off to the bathroom in a restaurant to pay a bill before we could argue with him. But most importantly, he was generous with his time. If you needed anything, Keith would stop what he was doing to help you out. I remember one time in particular, Lyle was out of town and Nolan was supposed to dress in a shirt and tie for hockey. I had no clue how to tie a tie. I called Keith. He was at a neighbor's, but without a moment of hesitation, he said, "I'll be right there." He never made you feel bad, he always had a way of making you feel like there was no place he'd rather be.

Spencer really lucked out. He got to be part of many of his Papa's "tours" in the community. He got to watch him run errands, help out, always offer whatever was needed wherever it was needed without a second thought.

After Keith passed away, I noticed Spencer really wanting to help out. He joined the youth council, he started helping at the community rink, he volunteered at Namao Days and at the Canada 150 Celebration.

We never asked him to do these things...he asked us.

It was like in an instant I saw Keith in Spencer. It is like we have a piece of Keith back in our lives. This is the gift Keith left. His legacy lives on in all of us. How blessed we all are to have known and loved him.

Reflection:
What is ONE key learning that you can you take
away from this story?

"Success is not final, failure is not fatal; it is the courage to continue that counts."

Winston Churchill

DAY 16

Value words to focus on for today:
Achievement
Success
Excellence
Wealth

Sit in silence and think about what each of these words means to you.
Jot down your thoughts or write your own definition of each word:

Achievement -

Success-

Excellence -

Wealth -

Circle any word(s) that resonates for you:
Achievement   Success   Excellence   Wealth

If none of the above words resonate for you...move on to day 17.

What would a 10/10 day look like living this value?
Describe it in as much detail as you can.
Write, doodle, draw, be as creative as you wish.

Achievement Enriches My Life
by Thérèse deChamplain-Good

Coming to know my core values, not simply the ones that were passed on to me by my parents and family, helped me to truly understand who I am and what makes me happy.

Achievement, for some, is not a value and for many years I have been criticized for my strong motive to achieve. Knowing that I value achievement and that it is a good thing has helped me to be proud of the goals I have set for myself and achieved. This clarity allows me to set goals, speak my truth, and truly be happy for what I am accomplishing.

This quote says it all:

"True happiness comes from achievement, not luck. The road to happiness is paved with a thousand small accomplishments, each one of which enriches our lives and makes us better people."

Reflection:
What is ONE key learning that you can you take away from this story?

"Hope is being able to see that there is light despite all of the darkness."

Desmond Tutu

DAY 17

Value words to focus on for today:
Enthusiasm
Encouragement
Optimism
Hope

Sit in silence and think about what each of these words means to you.
Jot down your thoughts or write your own definition of each word:

Enthusiasm -

Encouragement -

Optimism -

Hope -

Circle any word(s) that resonates for you:

Enthusiasm   Encouragement   Optimism   Hope

If none of the above words resonate for you...move on to day 18.

What would a 10/10 day look like living this value?
Describe it in as much detail as you can.
Write, doodle, draw, be as creative as you wish.

For Me, the Choice is Optimism

by Jeunesse Pearson
Counsellor & Life Coach

For me optimism is so much deeper than just positive thinking, rose coloured glasses or pie in the sky daydreams. It is a central core value that when I am out of alignment, my life starts to unravel and things begin to feel hopeless and out of control. Optimism is hope. Optimism is faith. A belief that this beautiful life I have is going according to a greater plan. It does have a spiritual feel to it. By focusing on the positive, even if that means being positive that the pain I am currently in is for a greater purpose and will serve me somehow, gives me a calm and peaceful mind. I can then accept and move forward with a confidence and certainty I don't get when I let my mind go to fear, worst case thinking and catastrophe. Optimism is a way of keeping myself mentally well; it is a spiritual practice of sorts for me. I don't always get it right, and there are many times I get off course, but I can catch it, refocus and make the choice to see the situation in a more favorable light. Not suppressing it, not avoiding it, but moving through the emotions and knowing it will all be okay. Scientific studies have proven that we really do have a choice, learned optimism or learned helplessness. For me, the choice is optimism.

Reflection:

What is ONE key learning that you can you take away from this story?

"Home is not a
place…
it's a feeling."

Unknown

DAY 18

Value words to focus on for today:
Family
Love
Home
Connection

Sit in silence and think about what each of these words means to you. Jot down your thoughts or write your own definition of each word:

Family -

Love-

Home -

Connection -

Circle any word(s) that resonates for you:
Family   Love   Home   Connection

If none of the above words resonate for you...move on to day 19.

What would a 10/10 day look like living this value?
Describe it in as much detail as you can.
Write, doodle, draw, be as creative as you wish.

What Impact Will You Leave?
by Lori Moores

When I think about love and connection it reminds me of a book I read many years back, Mitch Albom's 'The 5 People You Meet In Heaven'. This emotionally pulling story depicts a true demonstration of the need and desire for human connection through the main character's struggle to find meaning in his life. It further gives a sense of how important and impactful your energy is to every single person you meet throughout your lifetime, and how we have the power to either positively or negatively influence another person's life. We are all born with an innate sense of love and connection and through acts of kindness and genuine understanding can create a level of interconnectedness that will surpass what most experience on a day to day basis. I'll forever remember the reflective question one of my professors in university posed to our class full of energetic, aspiring teachers, "Children remember their best and their worst teachers and rarely remember the mediocre ones. You have the opportunity to create lasting impressions on the lives of children every day that you walk into the classroom. You need to decide if you want to be their worst experience or their best experience." This statement has stuck with me throughout my career and has solidified that our every day actions can and will create a lasting impact on those we meet. Since reading this book many years ago, I live my life with the purpose to find meaningful ways to connect with people. If we are able appreciate people for the gifts they have to offer and genuinely see, hear and value them, we will always be met with the same level of love, kindness and appreciation. "Vulnerability is the essence of connection and connection is the essence of existence." -Leo Christopher.

Reflection:
What is ONE key learning that you can you take
away from this story?

"I can do things you cannot, you can do things I cannot; together we can do great things."

Mother Teresa

DAY 19

Value words to focus on for today:
Collaboration
Cooperation
Teamwork

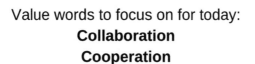

Sit in silence and think about what each of these words means to you. Jot down your thoughts or write your own definition of each word:

Collaboration-

Cooperation -

Teamwork -

Circle any word(s) that resonates for you:
Collaboration   Cooperation   Teamwork

If none of the above words resonate for you...move on to day 20.

What would a 10/10 day look like living this value?
Describe it in as much detail as you can.
Write, doodle, draw, be as creative as you wish.

Working Together for a Common Goal

by Danielle Reed

Teamwork is a value that for me, faded over time. When I was young, I absolutely loved playing sports. I loved playing for the sake of the game, but the truth is....I mostly played to be part of a team. I loved the deep connections that were formed when we, as athletes, came together to do something we loved. There was a trust and a loyalty that I felt every time I stepped on a court or a field. We had each others' backs. My happiest moments as a kid involved the times when I was playing sports. And my absolute favorite was when we would go to tournaments. Tournaments were where the real team bonding happened. It was where there were moments of seriousness but also lots of time for laughter and connection. Being part of a team was one of my greatest memories growing up.

As an adult, I continued playing sports, but by then it was all for the team aspect. I just loved spending time with amazing women and getting some exercise at the same time. I remember at the end of each season, feeling sad. I was never sad because we lost. I was mostly sad because from year to year the team always changed. You were never guaranteed to see the exact same faces on the field the following season.

Team - working together for a common goal and having fun while doing it meant the world to me.

In my career, I also did my best to create incredible teams. I tried to always make sure everyone on the team knew they mattered, felt valued and that we had time to have fun together. My teaching days meant more to me because I was surrounded by an amazing team.

Today, I am done with organized sports and I work for myself so a lot has changed. Sometimes, I miss being part of a team, but I am always grateful when I reflect on every one of the amazing teams I was lucky enough to be a part of.

I think my teams helped shape who I am today.

Reflection:
What is ONE key learning that you can you take
away from this story?

"Many of life's failures are people who did not realize how close they were to success when they gave up."

Thomas A. Edison

DAY 20

Value words for today:
Leadership
Perseverance
Ambition
Competitiveness
Challenge

Sit in silence and think about what each of these words means to you. Jot down your thoughts or write your own definition of each word:

Leadership -

Perseverance -

Ambition -

Competitiveness -

Challenge -

Circle any word(s) that resonates for you:
Leadership   Perseverance   Ambition   Competitiveness   Challenge

If none of the above words resonate for you...move on to day 21.

What would a 10/10 day look like living this value?
Describe it in as much detail as you can.
Write, doodle, draw, be as creative as you wish.

Sick and Tired of BLAH
By Danielle Reed

I had a client a while back. She is a seventeen year old girl. In my opinion she is one of the most amazing, honest, genuine people I have ever met. She came to see me because she was feeling like she was in a bit of a funk. I asked her to tell me what was going on in her life, and she began to describe it. The biggest struggle was that she felt unmotivated; like she wanted to climb back into bed most days. Nothing lit her up anymore. Everything felt like so much work! The first thing I did with her was the values exercise. As she described her most amazing days and shared things that frustrated her, I listened for the values that mattered to her. One that stood out to me was perseverance and hope. I asked her, "Do you think perseverance is important to you?" Without hesitation she said, "Absolutely!"

Then I said to her, "Do you see the disconnect? You value perseverance and yet you are in an unmotivated place in your life. When how you are living, and how you want to live are out of alignment, you tend to feel BLAH. My guess is that you are happiest when you are hopeful and persevering through the struggle."

She said, "That is totally it!" She then went on to say, "My whole life has been about perseverance. School hasn't come easy, and I've had to work really hard. I am happiest when I conquer things I didn't know I could. I like the feeling of achieving things that take work. I like to be hopeful."

My next question was, "What would it look like if you stepped into hope and perseverance right now? What would you do?"

She said, "I'd volunteer, I'd get a job and I'd get myself organized to start the next school year. Oh…and I'd come up with a phrase to keep myself on track." So together we came up with a plan…and just two weeks later this is what she was doing: 1. She started volunteering as a mentor in our Fit+Fierce program for the year. 2. She got a part time job. 3. She began to do a weekly Sunday ritual of planning her schedule for the week. 4. She came up with a mantra to remind herself to keep going and to persevere when things became challenging. This girl is rocking it! It isn't about BIG changes…it's about re-connecting with your values and re-aligning your life with what matters. I saw her last week and her smile and her energy were so different! It was like she found the best part of herself again!

Reflection:
What is ONE key learning that you can you take
away from this story?

"It is not the strongest of the species that survives, nor the most intelligent. It is the one that is most adaptable to change."

Charles Darwin

DAY 21

Value words for today:
Organization
Efficiency
Adaptability
Competency

Sit in silence and think about what each of these words means to you. Jot down your thoughts or write your own definition of each word:

Organization -

Efficiency -

Adaptability -

Competency -

Circle any word(s) that resonates for you:
Organization   Efficiency   Adaptability   Competency

If none of the above words resonate for you...move on to day 22.

What would a 10/10 day look like living this value?
Describe it in as much detail as you can.
Write, doodle, draw, be as creative as you wish.

Choosing to be In Control of My Life
By Denisa Rajská

For a long time, I believed that things would just happen somehow and that there was no need to be stressed out because there was no plan. That all changed when I came on a year long youth exchange to another country. I came to a place where planning and organization were a must. Not having a plan was disrespectful towards others in terms of needing a ride, knowing where I was at and other stuff. That was never something I wanted people to feel...disrespect. But it did take some time to actually understand why planning and organization was a good thing for me. First, I needed to convince myself that organization mattered to me. People would tell me it was, and I'd just mindlessly agree, but never act on it. Everything changed when I started to feel the frustration of things not working out because there was no plan. I was starting to feel what everyone around me must have felt. With time, I noticed how much taking a few minutes to plan my day and tell everyone about it did so much more than I thought. Communication got easier, and I could see it on the people around me. I could see that they were happier and less stressed when they knew my plans. Then suddenly, I didn't want to go out anymore without knowing all the facts; without having a single clue about what I was going to do. I still like to act spontaneously at times, but even then, I take a few minutes to think about what I am doing and how to make it work best. Being more organized has helped me to feel more in control of my life. Waking up in the morning is easier when I know what my day will be like. It allows me more time to enjoy the situations I am in. I still can't organize my closet that well, I'll admit that, but I have to keep at least one thing in chaos. I've learned a great deal about myself and the importance of organization in my life today. I used to think planning was no fun, but I've discovered that I actually like it and need it. I thought organized was for people that were too uptight, but I've come to realize that you can still have tons of fun and go on adventures while being organized. In fact they often turn out even better. It all kind of proved me wrong in the end, but sometimes that can be a good thing.

Reflection:
What is ONE key learning that you can you take
away from this story?

"A healthy outside starts from the inside."

Robert Urich

DAY 22

Value words for today:
Health
Balance

Sit in silence and think about what each of these words means to you.
Jot down your thoughts or write your own definition of each word:

Health -

Balance -

Circle any word(s) that resonates for you:
Health   Balance

If none of the above words resonate for you...move on to day 23.

What would a 10/10 day look like living this value?
Describe it in as much detail as you can.
Write, doodle, draw, be as creative as you wish.

I Was Miserable!

By Danielle Reed

For years, I constantly talked about wanting balance in my life. But I also held this strong belief that it would NEVER happen. So I existed in my own life. I woke up, jumped on the hamster wheel of overwhelm, jumped off late at night, slept, woke up and did it all over again. And I WAS MISERABLE. I remember the day I found my top values…I was trying my hardest to leave balance off the list. If I wasn't going to allow myself to have it, why put it on the list? But my heart was screaming at me. When life is balanced, you are happiest. When life is balanced, you are at your best. When life is balanced, you are able to give your best to those around you. I made a conscious decision to put BALANCE on my list. And then, I made a conscious decision to actually try to make it possible. This was so foreign to me. How could I ever do this? It took one step at a time. When people asked me to do things or sign up for things, I NEVER responded right away. I would say, "I'll let you know." Then I would sit and ask myself if this felt right. When it felt right to do it, my heart was calm and content. When it felt wrong, the pit of my stomach would feel yucky. So I began to say YES only when my heart felt the alignment. And it felt so good. When I said NO, I said it from a truly genuine place. I'd say something like, "I would love to do that; however, balance is really important to me and saying yes to that will tip the scales right now. I'm going to have to say no." It felt so honest and so good. I never imagined that a balanced life was something I was capable of having. Today, I know that it is an absolutely non-negotiable value for me. I am my best for myself and others when I choose balance.

Reflection:
What is ONE key learning that you can you take away from this story?

"Commitment is what transforms a promise into reality."

Abraham Lincoln

DAY 23

Value words to focus on for today:
Reliability
Accountability
Responsibility
Commitment

Sit in silence and think about what each of these words means to you.
Jot down your thoughts or write your own definition of each word:

Reliability -

Accountability-

Responsibility -

Commitment -

Circle any word(s) that resonates for you:

Reliability   Accountability   Responsibility   Commitment

If none of the above words resonate for you...move on to day 24.

What would a 10/10 day look like living this value?
Describe it in as much detail as you can.
Write, doodle, draw, be as creative as you wish.

Why Settle?

by Jen Traxel
The Intuitive Mermaid

I've spent the majority of my twenties seeking out as many opportunities as possible. I always considered myself a multi-passionate person with an endless bucket list of goals I'd strive to accomplish. From working in a salon as a hairstylist, training sea lions and working closely with marine life & exotic species in both a zoo & aquarium, being on the front lines as a police officer, 911 emergency communications and becoming an entrepreneur running my own business to name a few. I travelled the world - swimming with wild dolphins in the Bahamas, planting coral & becoming a yoga teacher in Bali, learning meditation in Sedona, climbing volcanos in Nicaragua, swimming with a mermaid tail in Hawaii, exploring the beaches of Portugal and scuba diving the blue hole in Belize. My life has been full of adventure, freedom and excitement! Although these incredible memories have been life-changing, as I approach the end of my twenties I realize there is a pertinent value word that has been missing. Despite the excitement of constant change, I feel so good when I'm simply at home with family, slowing down, grounding myself and not always striving for more. In essence the overall feeling in my life that I crave - in career, relationships, health, home & beyond - is to become more present, committed in the long term and grow some roots. The word commitment has always been a challenge for me; mostly because I always had the idea that to live a full life you "should never settle". What I've come to realize is that the more I commit to myself, my relationships, my career, my health and my home the more fulfilled I feel inside and out.

Reflection:
What is ONE key learning that you can you take
away from this story?

"The real gift of gratitude is that the more grateful you are, the more present you become."

Robert Holden

DAY 24

Value words to focus on for today:
Recognition
Time
Gratitude

Sit in silence and think about what each of these words means to you. Jot down your thoughts or write your own definition of each word:

Recognition -

Time -

Gratitude -

Circle any word(s) that resonates for you:
Recognition   Time   Gratitude

If none of the above words resonate for you...move on to day 25.

What would a 10/10 day look like living this value?
Describe it in as much detail as you can.
Write, doodle, draw, be as creative as you wish.

There Was No Longer Room for Depression

by Deanne Whittle

Gratitude is one of my core values! A few years back I suffered with depression, and I focused so much on anger & sadness! I decided to start a gratitude jar. I wrote things down daily and placed them in the jar. After a month I sat back and read everything I put in the jar, and they truly whispered to me that I needed to spend more time focusing on what I was grateful for! Since then, I have written down many small things that warm my heart and put a smile on my face and many long stories that are life long memories that I am so grateful for. I've discovered that this simple task makes me more aware of my feelings and what makes me happy. Things such as helping those in need and loving unconditionally are just a few examples of what makes me feel blessed! Gratitude brings me so much joy & happiness! I no longer have to write them down, I simply sit back and take the time each day to remind myself that I'm so grateful for my health, happiness & family and friends! I now know that I will always be grateful for this beautiful life and there's no longer room for depression! Gratitude will be a value for the rest of my life. The more I focus on it, the better life feels.

Reflection:
What is ONE key learning that you can you take
away from this story?

"Listen to silence. It has so much to say."

Rumi

DAY 25

Value words to focus on for today:
Silence
Simplicity
Relaxation
Peace
Calm

Sit in silence and think about what each of these words means to you.
Jot down your thoughts or write your own definition of each word:

Silence -

Simplicity -

Relaxation -

Peace -

Calm -

Circle any word(s) that resonates for you:

Silence   Simplicity   Relaxation   Peace   Calm

If none of the above words resonate for you...move on to day 26.

What would a 10/10 day look like living this value?
Describe it in as much detail as you can.
Write, doodle, draw, be as creative as you wish.

My Number One Value is Calm
by Erin Hettle

I took the Daring Way™ course where we learned our top 10 values and it helped me understand so much about myself. My number one value is CALM, and it helped me understand that when life is crazy or when my kids are screaming or yelling how it truly affects my overall mood. I explained this to my family one night and hoped that they may understand. From that day forward whenever life is crazy or my kids are screaming my son always says, "Sorry mom, we are stomping on your value." I love that he is aware of that now; that he understands me and tries to respect my values. Not long after, I got my What Matters™ cards as a birthday present and sat down with my family to help them learn more about their own values. After seeing my 14 year old son's values it helped me to be a better parent. He used to always smile or make a joke when he was in trouble or uncomfortable, and I never really understood. In fact I felt like a bad mom because it would make me get even more mad at him. I would be thinking, "How can he even think this is funny?" When he did his values and I looked at his first value on his list, it was humor. It made so much sense. He is such a funny kid, and he loves to make people laugh. So now when he is in trouble or uncomfortable I don't let that smile or joke bug me as I know it is a part of him. This has been a huge help in our relationship with each other. We try to stay true to our own values and not stomp on each other's values either. Knowing my values has had a huge impact on my life. It has truly made me understand myself and those around me so much more.

Reflection:
What is ONE key learning that you can you take
away from this story?

"To forgive is to set a prisoner free and discover that the prisoner was you."

Lewis B. Smedes

DAY 26

Value words to focus on for today:
Understanding
Forgiveness
Respect

~~~~~~

Sit in silence and think about what each of these words means to you.
Jot down your thoughts or write your own definition of each word:

Understanding-

Forgiveness -

Respect -

Circle any word(s) that resonates for you:
Understanding   Forgiveness   Respect

If none of the above words resonate for you...move on to day 27.

What would a 10/10 day look like living this value?
Describe it in as much detail as you can.
Write, doodle, draw, be as creative as you wish.

The Fine Line Between Love & Hate
Anonymous Author

Until recently I didn't think forgiveness was important, and it certainly never occurred to me that it would become one of my core values. ...until I stood on the fine line between love and hate. I hated how my husband betrayed me, yet I still loved him. How is that possible? I was right, he was wrong!   All this anger inside of me was like drinking poison, and hoping he would suffer. But the truth is, I was the one suffering. He wasn't. Therefore, I knew something had to shift, it was making me sick. I realized that standing on that line of love vs hate I had to step into forgiveness. I didn't want to. I fought it. I kicked and screamed. It felt so good to blame and condemn his behaviour. However, as I began the process of forgiving, I realized that it was not for him, it was really for me. When I allowed myself to truly forgive him, I was able to see my part, and therefore forgive myself. That was the hardest part. Admitting that I was an active participant, and having to let myself off the hook. Forgiveness isn't a noun, it's a verb. It's taking action to free oneself. To have peace. It cleans the slate of blame and guilt and remorse; that's a deadly cocktail. Forgiveness doesn't mean I condone his behaviour, I simply no longer allow his actions, or anyone's to poison my life. That's true freedom.

Reflection:
What is ONE key learning that you can you take
away from this story?

"A big part of
financial freedom
is having your
heart and mind
free from worry
about the what-
ifs of life."
Suze Orman

DAY 27

Value words for today:
Safety
Financial Security

Sit in silence and think about what each of these words means to you. Jot down your thoughts or write your own definition of each word:

Safety -

Financial Security-

Circle any word(s) that resonates for you:
Safety   Financial Security

If none of the above words resonate for you...move on to day 28.

What would a 10/10 day look like living this value?
Describe it in as much detail as you can.
Write, doodle, draw, be as creative as you wish.

No One Wants to Talk About Money
By Danielle Reed

Well...it only makes sense to end the values stories with a bit of humor. I put the call out for people to submit stories for this journal, and I did not receive a single one about financial security. I put a second and third call out and not a single response. It was getting close to the deadline for the book and I was feeling desperate. I asked my husband one night, "Do you value financial security at all? Even a little bit?" We both burst out laughing. You know how opposites attract? Well, Lyle and I are opposites in so many ways, but when it comes to money we have the same mindset....spend it!

As we were laughing, it got me thinking about my money mindset and why I do not value financial security. I mean don't get me wrong, I'm not financially irresponsible either, but I don't focus on saving for a rainy day. Lyle and I often laugh as we talk about retirement. We are both self-employed and we worry that someday when we can no longer work, we may have to move in with friends or family. Our kids may be a bit terrified with the thought of us living with them forever.

But the truth is, Lyle and I both have values that matter more to us. That's just the plain truth. Lyle values adventure and so anytime there is an opportunity for another "trip of a lifetime" on his motorcycle or a trip to LaPaz with our family he never gives it a second thought. He's ALL IN! We will make it work!

For me, I value optimism. I have this deep belief that everything will work out. That we will be fine. I don't lose sleep over money. I don't save for a rainy day. I just trust that we are responsible enough that it will all work out. And I sure hope I am right.

So for now, we are optimistically enjoying every minute of this life and it feels right for both of us!

Reflection:
What is ONE key learning that you can you take
away from this story?

What are YOUR Top Ten Values?

DAY 28

Reflect about the last 27 days.
Which TEN value words most resonate for you?
Write them below.

Values Manifesto

Take each of your ten value words and describe it.
Each word is so personal. It's your own interpretation of what it means and looks like in your own life. When you get clearer about what each value means, you can step more fully into living it with intention.

Here's mine:

Authenticity - I will choose to be me. To own my whole story. To be real.

Balance will always guide my decisions. My family will always come first.

Connection - I need connection way more than you may realize.

Gratitude - I love my life and thank you's mean a lot to me.

Humor is my gift but also my armor when my feelings get hurt please notice which one it is.

Health - Working out really does make me happy!

Learning - I love to learn and I love to take my learning and teach others.

Organization - I don't need sparkling. I just like things in their places.

Optimism - I do believe anything is possible. Negativity drains me.

Understanding - I need you to take time to "get" me and I will do the same for you.

Legacy - I am committed to leaving an impact in this world in my message, but mostly through the example I am to my kids.

Values Manifesto

Time to write your own manifesto

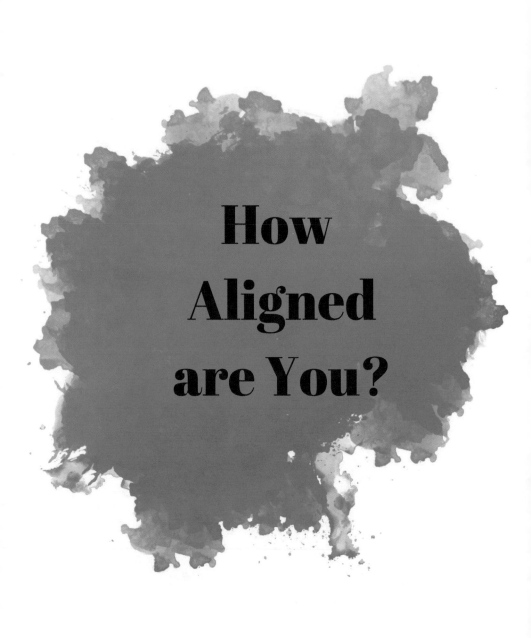

How
Aligned
are You?

DAY 29

As you look at each of your value words, ask yourself,
"Am I living in alignment with this value right now?"

Value   Am I living this value right now?

1.

2.

3.

4.

5.

6.

7.

8.

9.

10.

Reflection:

Take a few minutes to journal about which values are aligned and why, which values are not aligned and why, and what you want moving forward.

"Integrity is choosing courage over comfort; choosing what is right over what is fun, fast or easy; and choosing to practice our values rather than simply professing them."

Brené Brown

DAY 30

Living with Intention
Practicing our Values rather than simply professing them

Turn your values into a practice by simply completing the following:
Examples:
I value balance so I will only work three evenings per week.
I value connection so I will have two meaningful conversations a week.
I value gratitude so I will write one thank you card each day.

I value _____ so I will _____

I value _____ so I will _____

I value _____ so I will _____

I value _____ so I will _____

I value _____ so I will _____

I value _____ so I will _____

I value _____ so I will _____

I value _____ so I will _____

I value _____ so I will _____

I value _____ so I will _____

Thank you

I would like this opportunity to say thank you.
Thank you to the brave contributors in this book. It took courage to
share your story, and I am forever grateful.
Thank you to you for purchasing the book and believing in the work
of values which I am so passionate about.
Thank you to my family and friends who support me every step of
my journey. I am so blessed to have you in my life.
And of course, thank you to Lyle, Nolan & Spencer. You are my WHY.
You are the ones who made me realize that living a life
of intention was the way home to the real me.

For more information about Values and my work go to:
www.coachonthego.net
https://www.facebook.com/coachonthego.net/

Made in the USA
Columbia, SC
28 May 2018